Title IV Funded

ST. JOSEPH'S SCHOOL

WOODLAND ANIMALS

Woodland Animals

*written and photographed
by George A. Smith*

Abelard-Schuman
London New York Toronto

Also by George A. Smith: *Hatch and Grow* (with Ivah Green)

Copyright © text and photographs 1970 by George A. Smith
Library of Congress and Catalogue Card Number: 75-123520
Standard Book Number: 200.71698.0

London	New York	Toronto
Abelard-Schuman	Abelard-Schuman	Abelard-Schuman
Limited	Limited	Canada Limited
8 King St.	257 Park Ave. S.	200 Yorkland Blvd.
WC2	10010	425

Printed in the United States of America
Designed by Werner Brudi
An INTEXT Publisher

Contents

List of Photographs		7
Introduction		9
Part I	Mammals	11
Part II	Reptiles	50
Part III	Amphibians	70
Part IV	Birds	87
Index		126

List of Photographs

White-tailed deer (fawn)   13
Eastern cottontail   15
Meadow vole   17
Muskrat   19
White-footed mouse   19
Flying squirrel on tree trunk   21
Flying squirrel about to glide   22
Red squirrel   24
Baby gray squirrels   25
Gray squirrel   26
Eastern chipmunk   28
Adult woodchuck   30
Young woodchucks   31
Bobcat   33
Gray fox   35
Gray wolf   37
Striped skunk   39
Raccoon on tree   40
Raccoon about to descend tree   42
Sleeping big brown bat   44
Young brown bats sleeping   45
Star-nosed mole   47
Opossum   49
Black rat snake   53
Black rat snake eggs   54
Ringneck snake   55
Hognose snake blowing up its neck   57
Hognose snake flashing its tongue   58
Hognose snake in pretended convulsion   58
Hognose snake being picked up   59
Hognose snake looking around   60
Hognose snake crawling away   60
Fence lizard   62
Box turtle   65
Bog turtle   67
Snapping turtle   69
American toad   73
Male toad with blown-up throat, singing   74
Female and male toad during egg laying   75
Tiny black tadpoles   75
Toad tadpole with legs beginning to show   76
Toad ready to leave water   76
Leopard frog   78
Tree frog   80
Bullfrog   82
Red-backed salamander   85
Long-tailed salamander   86
Song sparrow   89
Song sparrow nest   89
Three baby buntings in nest   91
A baby bunting on tree limb   91
Baby bunting being fed   92
Mother shoving bug all the way down baby's throat   93
Ovenbird in front of nest   95
Wood thrush   97
Brown thrasher female on nest   99
Young brown thrasher   99
Male brown thrasher   100
Tufted titmouse   102
American crow   104
Yellow-shafted flicker   106

7

Ruby-throated hummingbird   108
Hummingbird's nest   109
Hummingbird babies in nest   109
Screech owl   111
Barn owl on nest in chimney   113
Baby barn owls   114
Young sparrow hawk   115
Young sparrow hawk learning to fly   116
Pet sparrow hawk with author   117
Mallard mother and ducklings "freezing" for self-protection   119
Adult mallards in water   120
Mallards "tipping up" in water for food   120
Canada geese in V-formation in water   122
Goose being held by boy rescuer   122
Green heron   124
Great blue heron   125

Introduction

A walk in a woods can be an exciting adventure. Where trees grow dense and tall and the ground around is covered with a deep and rich carpet of leaves, you will discover a world of animal wonders. Deer, raccoons, squirrels, and white-footed mice live in the woods, as well as snakes, turtles, frogs and salamanders.

Warblers, wrens and thrushes stake out sites in which to sing their songs, build their nests and rear their young. Woodpeckers, hawks and owls live in the woods, where spreading trees offer protection for them and their families.

A woods for exploration need not be a deep forest or a dense wilderness. A few acres of natural woodland containing a pond or a stream can provide endless hours of fascinating observation.

In preparing yourself for a woodland exploration, dress comfortably and wear shoes designed for hiking. If you wish, take along field guidebooks to the common American species of birds, mammals, reptiles and amphibians, so that you will be able to identify the animals you will see.

While attempting to observe woodland animals, it is important to remember that quietness contributes a lot to your success. Choose a comfortable place from which a clear vision is afforded, one from which you might be fortunate enough to see an animal before it sees you. Wild animals, as a rule, are afraid of human beings and will seek cover at the first sight of a person. Look and listen in all directions for any unusual disturbance. Often the rustling of a dead leaf or the trembling of low-growing plants will point out the exact spot to be watched for a small animal, such as a vole or a white-footed mouse. Larger animals, such as foxes and raccoons, sometimes are seen in daytime, ambling through the woods in search of something to eat. Even after dark, the many woodland creatures that are more or less nocturnal may be seen with the aid of a strong flashlight. By far the best time to observe most amphibians is at nighttime.

If you are quiet, and look carefully, and do not disturb the woodland life around you, your patience will be rewarded—after all, that's how the photographs in this book were made! Good luck.

George A. Smith

Part 1

Woodland Mammals (Mammalia)

Woodlands, especially those that are natural and extensive, generally contain a number of mammals—warm-blooded animals that nurse their young. Observing animals in their natural environments usually provides much more information than can be obtained by seeing them at a zoo.

Most animals are harmless when encountered in the woods, unless they are cornered or trying to protect their young. However, as a safety precaution, it is always best to avoid rushing in too suddenly and too closely when a wild animal is encountered. Binoculars are helpful in observing wild animals from a safe distance.

Classification of common woodland mammals:

1. Hoofed mammals with even toes (Artiodactyla): deer, sheep, goats.
2. Mammals with two pairs of upper incisors (Lagomorpha): rabbits and hares.
3. Gnawing mammals (Rodentia): muskrats, woodchucks, squirrels, mice.
4. Flesh eaters (Carnivora): skunks, foxes, raccoons, bobcats.
5. Mammals with membranous wings (Chiroptera): bats.
6. Insect eaters (Insectivora): moles and shrews.
7. Pouched mammals (Marsupialia): opossums.

White-tailed Deer
Odocoileus virginianus

One of the most beautiful action scenes of all the great outdoors is that of a herd of white-tailed deer bounding through the woods. When alarmed, these graceful and fleet-footed animals, with their heads and tails held high in the air, run away with amazing speed. A white-tail can leap a distance of twenty feet. In bounding, its hind feet reach ahead of its front feet, with its dewclaws striking the ground.

The family life of the white-tailed Virginia deer is unusual. At birth a baby deer or fawn weighs from three to five pounds, and is only about a foot and a half tall. It is covered with a brown, dappled coat that helps camouflage it from the sharp eyes of foxes, coyotes, and other predators. It lies motionless in a bed of brown leaves, usually at the base of a tree, until its legs are strong enough to carry it through fields and woodlands. For a year or more a young deer remains under the care of its mother, usually traveling by her side until it is practically full-grown. Even after that time, deer usually graze and travel in groups

A male deer or buck grows antlers that curve forward and inward with unbranched tines or prongs. The antlers are shed annually after the mating season, which usually occurs during the winter season. From spring until fall, during the time a buck is growing new antlers, he is shy, timid, and solitary in his habits. The antlers, while growing, are soft and furry—"in velvet."

The white-tailed deer feeds on grass and low-growing leaves and twigs of deciduous trees. In winter, when food is scarce, it eats buds, berries, mosses, and lichens. White-tailed deer do well in almost any wooded range where there is sufficient browsing food and a good supply of running water.

White-tailed deer (fawn)

Eastern Cottontail
Sylvilagus floridanus

Cottontail rabbits have survived and multiplied down through the ages by evolving successful ways of evading enemies and by producing several litters a year.

Baby cottontails, usually five in number, are born in a mere depression in a plot of grass or weeds. They are concealed by nothing more than a thin blanket of grass and fur from the mother's body, which she spreads over them when she leaves the nest. While young and helpless, baby rabbits also lack odor, which helps to protect them.

Hares differ from rabbits in that the female builds no nest. Young hares, known as leverets, are active soon after birth. Jack rabbits and hares are larger and have longer ears than cottontails.

Few animals are as playful as cottontails. In the evening several will run in circles, and roll over and tumble as if playing games. But at the first suspicious sound they snap to attention, stiffen their long ears, and brace their hind legs for a sudden getaway. As soon as danger comes too close, they are off with a leap, warning their fellows with their bobbing cottontails.

Eastern cottontail

Meadow Vole
Microtus pennsylvanicus

The meadow vole, also called meadow or field mouse, is found in varying forms throughout most of North America. It is a small rodent of the same family as mice, rats, and lemmings. This rather stocky mouse-like creature, about six inches in length, has short ears, and black beady eyes. The color of the fur varies from a silvery gray to a reddish brown, depending on the sub-species and the geographical location. Western voles are grayish in color, while those of the east tend to be more brownish in color.

Voles live on the ground in grassy fields and open woodland, where they travel through partially concealed runways. They do not hibernate in winter but feed the year round on grass, seeds, bark, and roots. They live in nests constructed from plant material, which are placed under some protection such as a heavy tuft of grass or a fallen piece of a tree. Meadow voles are prolific breeders. One pair may produce several litters a year, with an average of six in each litter. In turn, the young mature rapidly and may leave the nest in a few weeks and be ready to rear families of their own. Fortunately, such a population explosion is kept under control by predatory animals. Hawks, owls, foxes, and bobcats thrive on a steady diet of the rodents. Much of the food of a common straying house cat consists of meadow voles.

A meadow vole.

Muskrat
Ondatra zibethicus

The muskrat, resembling an overgrown field mouse, is a valuable furbearing rodent occurring throughout most of the United States. It is a robust animal weighing up to four pounds with dense brownish fur and a somewhat scaly tail. In every respect it is well adapted for the aquatic life it leads. A muskrat is at home in fresh and salt-water marshes, rivers, ponds, and lakes, where it feeds on aquatic vegetation. It burrows into stream banks and builds beaverlike houses in swamps and lakes. A swimming muskrat looks like a small beaver, except that it does not have the beaver's paddle-shaped tail; a muskrat's fourteen-inch tail is vertically flattened and is used like a ship's rudder.

The home of a muskrat is uniquely constructed for comfort and protection. Several types of homes are constructed, depending on the nature of the environment. Muskrats living along the banks of farmland streams build dens in soil above water level, but with the entrance from the stream below water level. A ground opening, especially for ventilation, may be loosely plugged with vegetation. Marsh-dwelling muskrats build dome-shaped homes rising above the water, with an entrance below water level. These mounds, built of dead cattail stalks and mud, resemble small haystacks and are easily spotted from a distance. A den serves principally as a sleeping room and nursery. A litter of from five to seven muskrat babies is raised each year. The young are sometimes seen swimming along a stream in daylight; the adults are generally nocturnal in their habits.

The muskrat is one of the most important fur-producing animal in America. Enormous numbers are trapped each year, mostly for the pelts, which reach the market under the label Hudson seal. The finished fur, usually dyed black, is warm and handsome. The flesh of the animal makes a tasty dish and is served under the name of "marsh rabbit." Few would relish the idea of eating rat meat, for that is exactly what it is—a rat with a musky odor.

Muskrat

White-footed mouse

White-footed Mouse
Peromyscus lecopus

A gentle rustle in the evening in fallen leaves tells you that a white-footed mouse probably is foraging for food. Under cover of darkness, this elfin creature with beady eyes and a spotless robe of fawn and white evades many of its enemies that would like to catch it.

This mouse, a nocturnal animal, sleeps during the day and comes out at night to find grass seeds, small nuts, and insects. It is especially fond of beechnuts. Like the chipmunk, white-foot gathers food in the fall and caches it away to be eaten during the lean days of winter.

The white-footed mouse, differing from the house mouse (*Mus musculus*), prefers to live in the woods where it finds material that will make its dwelling cozy and warm. Milkweed floss, rabbit fur, and dry grasses are combined to build a nest in a hollow tree. Sometimes a discarded bird's nest, suitably located in a bush, is arched over on the top to provide a nest. The white-foot raises several litters, with an average of four in each, in the course of a year.

A flying squirrel pauses on a tree trunk.

Flying Squirrel
Glaucomys volans

The flying squirrel, from the free translation of its scientific name, is a silver-gray mouse that flies. This little squirrel, about the size of a mouse, does not have flying wings like a bird, but it is equipped by nature to glide from one tree trunk to another. Its gliding equipment consists of a fold of loose, furred skin extending along its sides from its front to its hind legs, with paws free for normal use.

This attractive little creature wears a thick coat of soft, glossy fur, olive-brown above and white below. Its beady night-seeing eyes are circled with black. Its flattened tail, about four inches long, aids the flying squirrel in directing its glide.

To see a flying squirrel in daytime going through its sensational gliding act, you should tap briskly on a tree containing deep woodpecker holes. If a flying squirrel is sleeping inside, it usually comes out to see what is going on. When alarmed, up the trunk it races, then leaps into the air and with the fold of skin stretched between its out-flung legs, it glides safely to the base of a more distant tree. The average distance covered by each flight is around a hundred feet.

The flying squirrel's nest is generally in a deserted woodpecker hole. It is lined with shreds of bark, dry leaves, and softer material, such as feathers and fur. The nest is usually located near water, where the little creature can find a refreshing drink each night while foraging for food. Its daily food includes seeds and nuts, buds and berries, insects and insect larvae.

Flying squirrels raise from one to two families annually. From three to six are born in each litter. The young need no coaching to learn to glide. They instinctively take to the air like ducklings to water.

A flying squirrel about to glide from a tree.

Red Squirrel
Tamiasciurus hudsonicus

An active resident of the woods is the little red squirrel who goes about its business of scampering through trees all day long and well into the evening. When you invade its domain, this aggressive little squirrel, measuring about a foot from the tip of its nose to the tip of its tail, becomes frantic. Jerking its long, bushy tail and stamping its tiny, furred feet, it defies and defames you with its expressive vocabulary. From its chattering call, the red squirrel has been given the appropriate name of chickaree.

At the first hint of danger, especially when a hawk is present, the red squirrel leaps to the occasion. If it is on the ground, it races away as fast as its springy feet can carry it; if attacked in a tree, it gallops over branches with fore and hind feet moving in pairs. Sometimes the animal loses its grip and falls to the ground. Apparently it lands without injury, for in an instant it is up and away to the nearest hollow tree for protection.

From one to two families, averaging four in each, are raised annually. The nest of dry leaves and shredded bark may be placed in a natural tree cavity, a woodpecker hole, or in a burrow in the ground. Sometimes a spherical nest about a foot in diameter is placed in a clump of grapevines.

Red squirrel

Gray Squirrel
Sciurus carolinensis

The gray squirrel, with its graceful lines, flashing black eyes, and its elegantly plumed tail, is easily the best known and friendliest creature of the woods. It is also a favorite small-game quarry of woodland hunters.

Few animals are better equipped for living in the woods. With its long, needle-sharp toenails and powerful leg muscles, the gray squirrel is capable of cutting spirals up and down a tree trunk as fast as one's eyes can follow.

A gray squirrel's diet includes many kinds of nuts, berries, acorns, and mushrooms. A squirrel deftly holds a hard nut in its front paws to open it. Then with its chisel-sharp incisors, it cuts directly into the tasty kernel. Surplus nuts are hidden away in autumn to be eaten in winter.

In addition to filling tree cavities, the gray squirrel has the habit of burying nuts and acorns here and there in the ground. Among the many never retrieved, some take root and in time grow into valuable forest trees. The gray squirrel is the Johnny Appleseed of the forest.

These baby squirrels, gently placed on a tree trunk, show their instinctive urge to climb even before they are old enough to open their eyes.

A gray squirrel has an elegantly groomed, bushy tail.

Eastern Chipmunk
Tamias striatus

The little eastern chipmunk is everybody's friend until it becomes too friendly and begins sticking its nose into the picnic basket or finds its way into the cabin supplies. Then the little scamp is a friendly nuisance or a downright pest. It will stuff itself on cookies, bread, nuts, and fruit; then carry away in its expandable cheek pouches all the remaining food it can find. This it stores in its underground larder for future eating.

This little (five to six inches long, not counting its four-inch tail), brown-striped chipmunk is frequently seen sitting on a stump or a rock in or along the edges of woodlands. When alarmed, it runs, with tail held high, to its nearest hiding place in an underground burrow. The alarm call is a shrill, sharp *chip*.

The underground home of a chipmunk is extensive. For the first few inches, the burrow, only about two inches in diameter, goes down vertically, then it veers on a slope to the living chambers. Different rooms serve different purposes; several serve as storage quarters for food; another one is used as sleeping quarters; and still another room, the deepest one, is the toilet. By far the largest chamber, usually about a foot square, is the resting place where additional food, such as nuts and seeds, is stored under a mattress of dry grasses and shredded leaves. Chippy likes to eat his breakfast in bed in wintertime.

Eastern chipmunk

Woodchuck
Marmota monax

The woodchuck or groundhog came into prominence as a weather prophet when the early settlers came to America. In Europe it was the custom to associate the hedgehog with the weather conditions. Finding no hedgehogs in this country, the settlers just naturally gave the job of being weatherman to the groundhog from its resemblance to the hedgehog.

Naturalists have observed that the groundhog, famed weather prognosticator on Groundhog Day, February 2, is not at all concerned about seeing its shadow. At that time in winter, the groundhog is all rolled up in a ball under the ground. It usually comes out of hibernation around the middle of March.

The woodchuck is a robust animal, weighing about ten pounds, with a blunt nose, small quizzical eyes, and short tail. Its coat of long, coarse hair is grizzly brown; its cheeks and throat are somewhat lighter than the rest of its body.

If unmolested, the woodchuck grows up by feeding on green stuff and wild berries. Often a chuck is seen stretching up on its hind legs and holding the pose for minutes as it surveys the area for any hint of danger. When an enemy is seen, this alert animal snorts out a shrill whistle and quickly heads for its nearby burrow hole.

By the time the north wind begins to blow bitterly, a chuck is fat, cold, and drowsy. Then down into its burrow it waddles, and curls up into a furry ball to sleep away the cold months of winter.

Occasionally the woodchuck awakes from hibernating sleep, takes a few gulps of air to expand its lungs, then again falls into deep slumber to await the call of spring. When aroused by warm weather, the woodchuck ambles out of its underground quarters, blinks in the sunlight, yawns, stretches, and then sets out again for its long-awaited foraging excursion.

Young woodchucks.

An adult woodchuck.

Bobcat
Lynx rufus

The word lynx is from the Greek and applies to a kind of wildcat having relatively long legs, a stubby tail, and tufted ears. The bobcat, found throughout most of the wooded parts of the United States, is commonly known as the bay lynx. It is a close relative of the Canadian lynx (*Lynx canadensis*).

Recently I had an opportunity to observe a bobcat that was kept in a cage. As soon as I approached the animal, it assumed a catlike crouch with all four feet beneath it, showing its long, sharp teeth as if ready to spring at me instantly. Its piercing eyes were fixed on me. Ancients spoke of the eyes of a lynx as being strong enough to see through a stone wall. This bobcat, weighing about thirty pounds, resembled a big striped tomcat. Its fur was reddish with irregular black stripes. Its bulging stomach was white, beautifully marked with dark spots.

Game hunters frequently have exciting stories to tell about bobcats. The closest encounter I ever had with a bobcat was years ago while several companions were with me on a nighttime hunting trip in the mountains of Pennsylvania. I was sitting quietly on a log in pitch darkness waiting for my companions to join me when suddenly a bobcat let out a piercing call. I couldn't see the cat but I knew it was nearby. Apparently its fierce intentions soon subsided and it decided to go away. Like most wild animals, the bobcat will not attack a human being unless cornered or in defense of its young. In a fight, a bobcat can lick an average dog. In catlike fashion, it lies on its back and rakes the dog's face with its needle-sharp claws.

A bobcat eats rabbits, squirrels, birds, and sometimes a fawn. It hunts at night and stalks its prey by sight and smell. The pupils of its eyes enlarge in darkness like those of a house cat. The young, usually three, are born in the spring in a den in a rocky ledge or in dense underbrush. They are known as kits and have about the same habits as growing kittens, except that their playful games include more hisses, growls, and scratches.

This caged bobcat was a vicious-looking animal. It bared its teeth and squatted in readiness to spring at me as I moved toward it for a closeup photograph.

Gray Fox
Urocyon cinereoargenteus

The gray fox is a salt-and-pepper gray colored animal weighing around eight pounds. It has a beautiful face set off with white fur on the inside of its sharp-pointed ears, and on its cheeks and throat. Its sides, legs, and feet are reddish brown; its long, bushy tail is marked with a wide black line on the upper side.

The range of the gray fox extends throughout the eastern half of the United States and on into the southwestern area to the Pacific coast. It uses the same cunning as the red fox (*Vulpes fulva*), and feeds on birds and small mammals, especially mice and other small rodents. Berries and fruit also are included in its diet. Three to five cubs, resembling kittens, are born in the spring in a den tunneled into the ground in woodlands. The location is usually concealed under vines and brush.

Hunters say that the gray is not as crafty as the red fox, tires more quickly and when chased by hounds, tries to find protection in bushy woodlands; it will sometimes climb a tree for protection. From its climbing ability, the gray fox is often referred to as the "tree fox."

Gray fox

Gray Wolf
Canis lupus

The wolf for centuries has been associated with cunning and almost human intelligence. It is recorded that the Indians had such high regard for this wild animal that they frequently used the name of wolf in various combinations for their wisest and most cunning warriors. Names like Red Wolf and Black Wolf were common.

Before the white men came to these shores, the gray wolf, commonly known as the timber wolf, roamed over most parts of North America. But the wolf, like the Indian, was gradually reduced in numbers by the settlers who came to America. The few wolves remaining in the United States today have retreated to the remotest parts of the country. It seems unfortunate that a wild animal, so noted for its strength, endurance, cunning, and agility is now rarely seen except in a zoo or a wild animal preserve.

Recently I visited a game farm where I found the beautiful timber wolf shown in the photograph. Naturally it was kept inside a strong cage, but I did have an opportunity to admire it at very close range. The color of its coat was a mixture of brown, black, and iron-gray; the hair in its coat was of a rough and hard texture, blended toward the roots with a kind of ash-colored fur. I was especially impressed with the wolf's eyes which opened in a slanting direction. I was warned by the caretaker to avoid getting too close to the bars of the cage. Captive wolves generally retain their suspicious disposition. After all, a wolf is a wolf and its natural inclination is to try to use its iron jaws on the body of an animal.

Like many vanishing predatory animals, the wolf had a useful place in the maintenance of the balance of nature. It prevented deer and other wild animals from multiplying too rapidly. It also helped in promoting stronger strains of animals by weeding out the old, the sick, and the weak.

The gray wolf, now almost extinct in the United States, may be seen in zoos. It is a trim-looking animal, resembling a shepherd dog.

Striped Skunk
Mephitis mephitis

In an evening ramble through fields and woods, you will frequently come across that independent fellow, the striped skunk. He is easily a marked creature on a moonlight night because of his glossy-black color, white stripes, and long furry tail.

Give a skunk wide passageway and it continues ambling along, stopping here and there awhile to nose and dig into the soil for bugs and worms. When a nest of eggs is found, the entire clutch is eaten on the spot.

Approach a skunk too closely and you can expect it to prepare for battle. First, it warns you by raising its tail high over its body and stamping on the ground with its front feet. If this is not enough to have you back away, the angry animal will suddenly swing its rear-end into position and spray you with a strong-smelling oil from the base of its tail. Several blasts of this "liquid fire" are enough to drive away most adversaries.

Skunks live in dens, usually under the ground. They may dig their own burrows or use burrows discarded by woodchucks and other animals. The nursery, lined with vegetation, contains an average of five young, which are born in the spring. The mother begins to take her family on nightly foraging trips when they are seven to eight weeks old. The young usually follow the mother in single file. Most families are disbanded by early autumn.

Striped skunk

A raccoon is an excellent tree climber.

Raccoon
Procyon lotor

Tracks resembling the imprints of a barefoot child in the soft ground along a woodland stream are almost certain to be those of the raccoon. This compact animal, weighing from fifteen to twenty pounds, is noted for its masked face, pointed nose, and ringed tail.

The raccoon's scientific name, *Lotor,* meaning "the washer," has been given to this native American mammal from its habit of washing food found along streams. In addition to feeding on aquatic animals, such as crayfish, the raccoon eats eggs and birds, fruits and vegetables.

This nocturnal prowler, looking like the bandit that he is, will raid cornfields adjacent to woodlands when corn is juicy and tender. He will even sneak into a farmer's poultry pen and take off with a squawking hen or rooster.

On warm summer days, a raccoon likes to take a sun bath while resting high up in a den tree. Often several will be found in the same tree, for these animals are socially inclined and are rarely seen alone. In winter they do not hibernate, but when the weather is very cold, they sleep inside hollow trees, rolled up close together for warmth.

A raccoon descends from a tree by using its sharp claws.

Big Brown Bat
Eptesicus fuscus

Among mammals, the bat is the only one with true flying ability. The big brown bat, widely distributed over North America, is a mouselike creature with big ears and black beady eyes. Its leathery wings, with a spread of around twelve inches, extend along its body all the way from the long fingerlike bones of the forelegs to the hind legs and then back to include the tail.

On wing early in the morning and again in the evening, the big brown bat soars and banks at terrific speed in its pursuit of flying insects for food. No matter what the weather, the hour, or its speed, the bat never seems to strike even the smallest obstruction, such as a telephone wire.

Scientists have found that the bat has an efficient sonar system for flight; as it flies, it emits extremely high-pitched squeaks. The echoes of these squeaks—when the bat approaches an object—warn it to change course.

When winter approaches the bat easily goes into hibernation. Its sleeping quarters may be a rocky cave, an opening in a building, or almost any place where the creature is protected from wind and weather.

This big brown bat was found in daytime, fast asleep while clinging to the branches of a grapevine.

Young bats sleep in some secluded place while their mother is away finding insect food. They hang by sharp claws on their hind feet.

Star-nosed Mole
Condylura cristata

The star-nosed mole, found living in damp meadows and moist woods, is a fantastic example of nature's specialization. It is distinguished from the common mole (*Scalopus aquaticus*) by the pink fleshy fringe at the end of its pointed nose, found on no other animal. In addition to its specialized nose, this mole, like moles in general, has powerful shoulders and broad digging claws on its forelegs. Since eyes and ears, as most animals use them, would only be in the way for a mole, these organs are not highly developed.

Compensating for the mole's lack of good eyes and ears is its extremely sensitive nose. The mole uses its nose in finding its food, which consists mostly of earthworms and small subsoil insects. In digging a tunnel, the mole works like a swimmer using breast strokes. It can dig a fifty-yard-long tunnel in a single night. That's a big bulldozing job for a five-inch-long animal weighing only about three ounces. A mole's nest, located at the end of a deep tunnel, is lined with grass and leaves. An annual litter of from two to five is born in the spring.

Star-nosed mole

Opossum
Didelphis marsupialis

The opossum is the only North American mammal that is provided by nature with a built-in baby incubator like that of the Australian kangaroo. The opossum, in addition to being our only pouched mammal (marsupial), is unusual in many other respects.

This droll-looking creature, with paper-thin ears, a cone-shaped nose, and a ratlike tail, has a mouthful of fifty teeth and a good digestive system. It eats bugs and berries, mice and moles, earthworms and snakes. The opossum is especially fond of persimmons. In the fall of the year, a persimmon tree full of ripening fruit is a favorite dining place for a hungry opossum. In climbing a tree, this animal uses its prehensile tail to advantage. With the end of its tail wrapped around a sturdy limb, the opossum swings back and forth among under-hanging branches for fruity persimmons.

The opossum is a slow-moving animal and cannot always reach a tree when pursued by a dog. When cornered on the ground, it relies on its famous stunt of "playing dead." Even young opossums, as soon as they are old enough to walk, know how to "drop dead." Some naturalists say that the opossum probably faints from fear. Whatever the cause, the animal has an odd gift that it uses to advantage in its struggle for survival.

Opossum

Part 2

Reptiles (Reptilia)

Reptiles are cold-blooded animals with backbones. Most of them are covered with a modified skin structure made up of scales or bonelike plates. They breathe with lungs throughout their lives, even though some may spend all or part of their time in water. Most reptiles lay eggs on land; a few bear living young on land or in water. The young are sufficiently developed at birth to take care of themselves. Reptiles are more abundant in the tropics than they are in the temperate zones; they cannot survive freezing temperatures. Those living in climates with cold seasons hibernate below the frost line during winter.

Present-day reptiles are distinguished in that they belong to a class of lung-breathing vertebrates that have continued to live on earth for some 200 million years. However, many of them, including such mammoth creatures as dinosaurs, did not continue to survive the earth's major geologic and climatic changes. Proof of the existence of extinct reptiles is found in petrified skeletons that have been unearthed and displayed in museums.

Of the some 7,000 species of reptiles found in the world today, most of them live in the tropics. Less than 250 species are found within the borders of the United States. These include snakes, lizards, and turtles; also the few large lizardlike reptiles of the crocodile group, found only in the tropical rivers and marshes of the United States.

Snakes

These reptiles are crawling creatures that wriggle and slither over the ground because they have no legs for locomotion. In moving about, a snake uses the large single row of scales on the underside of its body, which are attached to its ribs with strong muscles. Besides lacking legs, snakes also lack ear openings and eyelids that move. Snakes hear by using their entire body to pick up vibrations through the ground.

A snake's long, forked tongue, which is entirely harmless, is flicked in and out through a groove in its upper jaw, to pick up dust particles that give it the sensation of both taste and smell. Snakes have small, hooked teeth, which are used to catch prey and to ward off enemies. Poisonous species have fangs, grooved or hollow, from which poison can be ejected. Snakes shed their skin, including the covering of the head and eyes, usually several times a year, by working their way out headfirst.

Snakes feed on live animals, which are swallowed whole. Each side of a snake's lower jaw moves separately, which makes it possible for a snake to swallow prey larger than the normal size of its mouth and throat. Snakes live mostly on rodents, frogs, rabbits, birds, and insects.

Poisonous snakes (copperheads, rattlesnakes, cottonmouths, and coral snakes) should be killed when they interfere with the well-being of people. There are, on the other hand, many species of non-poisonous snakes that are wantonly destroyed even though they are fascinating to observe and of great economic importance. Snakes in general are valuable allies of the farmer in helping him in his constant fight against destructive rodents, such as mice and rats.

Fortunately the many unfounded superstitions concerning snakes are no longer accepted as the truth. Today the number of people who appreciate snakes is growing through outdoor clubs, scouting organizations, and school instruction. But no one should approach a snake unless he can tell the poisonous species from the harmless ones.

Black Rat Snake
Elaphe obsoleta

The non-poisonous black rat snake is found in hilly woodlands from southern New England to Florida, and westward to Nebraska and into Texas. It is a heavy snake with keeled (or ridged) scales, a flat head and a short tail. Its average length is from four to five feet.

This snake is a good climber and is frequently found in shrubs and bushes. It even climbs into upper stories of buildings in woodland locations, especially in the fall when cold weather is approaching. The snake hunts for food at night. Residents in a building may hear it moving around; it is nocturnal in its habits.

In its nighttime hunting, the black rat snake destroys many rodents, such as mice and rats. It also preys on rabbits and other small animals, including birds. This snake is a true constrictor, and will quickly coil around and crush a vicious rat before attempting to swallow it. Small animals are not crushed, but swallowed alive.

In June or July the female deposits ten to twenty white, leathery eggs under heaps of leaves or in decaying logs. The young, brownish in color with dark blotches on the back, hatch in September or October. As they grow up and shed their skin from time to time, they become glossy black with a white chin and throat. They reach maturity in two to three years.

Holding a black rat snake, which is a true constrictor, should be done very carefully—as shown by this young man.

Ringneck Snake
Diadophis punctatus

The ringneck is an attractive little woodland snake found in the United States from Texas eastward to the Atlantic coastline. It is a slender snake, about a foot and a half long, with a flat head that is not distinct from its body. Where its neck should be, it wears a conspicuous yellow band of color. Its smooth-scaled cloak is steel gray above and yellow to reddish orange below. It hides during the day in moist woods under rocks and logs. At night it comes out to feed on insects, earthworms, and small salamanders.

The ringneck is harmless when picked up, except that it may try to gain its freedom by ejecting from its tail-end a foul-smelling fluid. Even though it is non-aggressive and easily tamed, this snake should not be kept in captivity for more than a day or so; it usually will not eat and soon dies of starvation.

The white, leathery eggs of the black rat snake.

Ringneck snake

Hognose Snake
Heterodon platyrhinos

The harmless hognose snake, reaching four feet in length, has a heavy body and a nose that is noticeably upturned. Its color varies from black to gray, often with blotches of color suggesting the poisonous copperhead. A dark phase occurs, in which the snake is practically all black above, but gray on the underside.

When the hognose is disturbed, it puffs out its neck, hisses, and lunges forward—but it never bites. If these menacing actions fail, it plays dead by rolling over and letting its tongue hang out. As soon as it senses that it is safe from danger, the hognose uprights itself and escapes as fast as it can to a safer location.

The hognose is a burrowing snake, usually found in dry sandy areas. It feeds on toads and frogs. The female lays several dozen thin-skinned eggs under some sort of protection, such as soil or vegetation. The young hatch in August and, like the adults, hibernate during the winter.

The harmless hognose snake at first glance looks like the poisonous copperhead. Its upturned nose is its distinguishing characteristic. When approached, it blows up its neck and arches its head like the poisonous cobra of India. At the same time it gives out a loud, hissing sound.

At close range, the hognose strikes at its intruder as it flashes its long tongue in and out of its mouth. It is only bluffing—it never strikes anyone.

If all this pretended attack fails, the snake will go into a spell of convulsions. It twists and turns, hangs its mouth, and rolls over on its back as if in a dying condition.

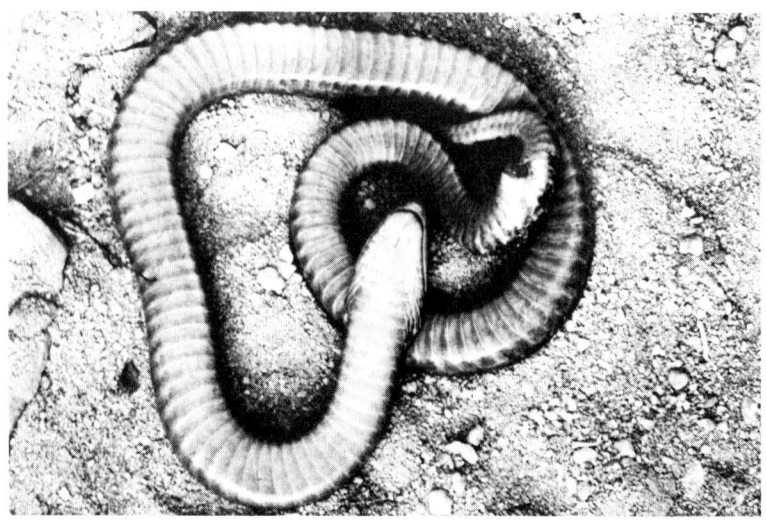

Pick up the "dead" snake, and it will eject a foul-smelling excreta. Its aim is accurate enough to force its tormenter to drop it to the ground.

Go away from the foul creature and watch for its next move. In about fifteen minutes it raises its head and looks around to see if the coast is clear.

If everything looks okay, the hognose quickly uprights itself and crawls away as fast as it can in search of a safer location.

Lizards

A lizard in general is defined as a scaly reptile with movable eyelids, ear openings, five clawed toes on each of four legs, and several rows of scales on the under side of its body. A few lizards, mostly those that burrow in the ground, have lost all traces of legs and are snakelike in appearance. Snakes, in fact, are closely related to lizards, and probably have evolved from ancient forms of lizards.

The class of reptiles known as lizards includes some 3,000 species. From the great diversity of lizards, they are divided into about twenty families, most of which live in the tropics. Less than a hundred species are found within the boundaries of the United States, and of these only two families, the iguanas and the skinks, are widely distributed.

Among the iguanas is the common eastern fence lizard (*Sceloporus undulatus*). This is the species of spiny scaled lizards most widely distributed through the United States and the one best known by most people.

Skinks are lizards with smooth, flat scales that produce a somewhat glossy appearance. These fast-running lizards are generally found in moist, wooded areas and are more or less terrestrial in their habits. The five-lined skink (*Eumeces fasciatus*) is common in woodlands throughout most of the eastern half of the United States.

Fence Lizard
Sceloporus undulatus

The little fence lizard, usually only about six inches in length, is one of our most widely distributed lizards. This dark gray, spiny-scaled member of the iguana family is found in dry woodlands and clearings from the Middle Atlantic States to Florida, and westward as far as Arizona.

Look for the fence lizard on warm, sunny days in summer. It is often seen sunning itself on fences, rocks, and logs. When disturbed on the ground, it usually dashes wildly for the nearest tree, where it climbs up a few feet and remains motionless. If approached, this artful dodger will quickly climb higher to the opposite side of the trunk. Such a performance may be repeated until the lizard is safely out of reach. The sight of a fence lizard racing along on the ground with its head held high easily suggests that of a miniature dinosaur.

Fence lizards have teeth on the inner surface of the jaws, which they use in catching their food, consisting mainly of insects and spiders. In summer an average of ten white, leathery eggs are laid in sandy soil or in rotten logs. The young, resembling their parents, hatch out in about two months. They grow up entirely on their own. Lizards are inactive on cool days and at night. They hibernate in the ground in wintertime to avoid freezing temperatures.

Fence lizard

Turtles

When you see a common box turtle you are looking at one of the most ancient of earth's land-living creatures, even older than the now extinct dinosaurs. The secret of the long survival of this ancient order of reptiles seems to be in their hard outer shells, and their simplified and unhurried mode of living.

Turtles are protected by a shell that is divided into two parts. The upper part or *carapace* covers the back; the bottom shell or *plastron* covers the underpart of the turtle's body. Through the opening of the two parts, the turtle can thrust its head, legs, and tail. The legs of sea turtles are modified into flippers for swimming, which are clumsy for use on land.

All turtles lay white, leathery eggs and bury them in the ground. Female sea turtles use their flippers in crawling out on land to lay their eggs. Under the heat of the sun, the eggs hatch into young that resemble their parents. From five to seven years are required for most turtles to reach maturity. Turtles have no teeth; they use their horny bills to cut their food into pieces that can be swallowed whole. Their food consists generally of animal life. Most species eat some plant food.

Scientifically these armored cruisers are divided into tortoises or land reptiles, terrapins or fresh-water reptiles, and turtles or sea reptiles. However, all are commonly known as turtles.

Box Turtle
Terrapene carolina

The common box turtle, found living in woodlands and moist fields, is a gentle, wild creature. Pick it up and about all it does is look at you with its beautiful red eyes, wiggle its legs, and probably hiss at you. Then quickly the turtle closes its shell so tightly you wonder how it can continue to breathe. It has some difficulty in closing its shell when it becomes too fat from over-eating such tasty items as mushrooms and wild strawberries. The box turtle also eats other food, such as insects, worms, and snails. In hot weather the turtle keeps cool by burrowing itself up to its head in soft, damp ground. It hibernates underground throughout the winter.

In the fall the female digs a hole a few inches deep in loose soil, where she lays four to eight eggs, with thin, white, flexible shells. After covering her eggs with soil, she leaves the scene with no further concern for her offspring. Plundering animals, such as skunks, dig into many nests and eat the eggs.

The young, about the size of a quarter, usually hatch in three months. Baby turtles have soft shells and must protect themselves by hiding under grass and debris. They are full-grown (about five to six inches long) by the time they are five years old. Box turtles have a long life-span of thirty or more years.

Box turtle

Bog Turtle
Clemmys muhlenbergi

This rare turtle, sometimes called the Muhlenberg turtle, after Dr. H. E. Muhlenberg, is found only in a few scattered areas of the eastern part of the United States. It is a turtle that lives in sphagnum bogs and wet lowlands, where it feeds on plants and small animals found above water as well as below.

The bog turtle is identified by a bright orange spot just back of each eye and by its brown-to-black upper shell, about four inches long and marked with concentric circles.

The two Muhlenberg turtles shown, a male and a female, were found in a bog only a few miles from the photographer's home in Quarryville, Pennsylvania. Dr. H. E. Muhlenberg did scientific field work in botany in the same bog where the turtles were found.

Bog turtle

Snapping Turtle
Chelydra serpentina

The turtle to be careful of is the savage fresh-water snapper, whose powerful cutting jaws can easily shear off a finger. When given a chance, it will lock its jaws on any part of your body and then hang on. Stay away from this turtle!

The snapper, one of our largest fresh-water turtles, is widely distributed from southern Canada to the Gulf of Mexico, westward to the Rocky Mountains. It eats fish, frogs, salamanders, ducklings—almost any animal it can catch in or on the water. It also eats carrion. Large prey, such as young muskrats, are dragged to the bottom of the stream and torn apart by its sharp claws and chopped into bits by its cutting jaws. Some plant food is included in a snapper's diet.

The female snapper leaves the water and crawls out on land to lay her eggs. She rarely travels more than a few hundred yards away from water. An average of twenty-five round, leathery eggs, resembling ping-pong balls, are buried in dry soil or sand. Baby snappers hatch out in the fall or the following spring. The little black-looking creatures, less than two inches in diameter, immediately head for water. They grow up slowly, depending on the food supply. Adults from ten to twenty years may weigh up to fifty pounds with shells measuring a foot or more in length.

Snapping turtle

Part 3

Amphibians (Amphibia)

The class of cold-blooded vertebrates that live a double life are known as amphibians. The term amphibian comes from two Greek words, *amphi,* meaning double, and *bies,* meaning life. Creatures, like toads, frogs, and salamanders, that live in water during the early part of their lives and on land as adults are classified as amphibians.

Amphibians differ from reptiles in that they are not covered with a scaly skin. They have a moist skin that is generally smooth in texture. Their feet also differ from those of reptiles; amphibians do not have claws on their toes. Amphibians in the first or larval stage of their development generally live in water and breathe with gills. In the second or adult stage, they breathe with lungs or through the skin. Some breathe with a combination of lungs and skin.

According to scientists, amphibians were the first vertebrates of some 350 million years ago that succeeded in leaving the water as adults to live on land. But even though these creatures as adults have developed a way to live on land, they usually return to the water to lay their eggs or, at least, they lay them in some moist place on land. In eggs laid on land, the transformation from larvae to adult takes place inside the egg.

Toads and Frogs

In general toads and frogs are a group of tailless amphibians that go through the first stage of their development while living in water as tadpoles. Toads have a warty skin and live mainly on land; frogs have a smooth skin and live in water or moist places, and are more athletic than their cousins, the toads.

There are about a hundred different species of these amphibians found in North America. Some live in wet lowlands, while others have extended their range into mountainous highlands. All North American species lay their eggs in water, generally in the spring of the year. During the egg-laying period, usually lasting only a few weeks, the males inflate their throats as they serenade the females with mating songs. The males clasp the females and fertilize the eggs externally as the eggs are laid in or on the surface of the water, depending on the species. Toads lay their eggs in long ropelike strings, while frogs lay theirs singly or in masses. The eggs are covered with a jellylike substance that absorbs water and keeps them afloat above the silt.

Usually within five to fifteen days, depending on the temperature of the water, gill-breathing tadpoles with long tails hatch from the eggs. For the most part, tadpoles of different species of toads and frogs look much alike. All generally feed on a vegetable substance found under water.

In the graduation of these amphibians from a life in the water to a life on land, lungs for breathing air are developed to take the place of gills. At the same time, legs suitable for land use are developed, while the tadpole tail is absorbed into the body. Some frogs are able to remain under water for long periods of time, especially during hibernation, by absorbing oxygen through the skin.

Toads and frogs eat food that is alive and active, which they catch by flicking out their long tongues covered with a sticky secretion. Their prey includes insects, worms, and other small creatures.

American Toad
Bufo terrestris

The common American toad lives on the land, except for the time that it goes into the water to mate and to lay its long strings of eggs, occurring in the spring just after it comes out of hibernation. During the few weeks toads live in water, they are beautiful creatures. They are clean and sparkling; their skin is a warm caramel color and their eyes are clear orbits flecked with gold.

It is during the mating season in the water that the males blow up their throats to immense proportions as they serenade the females. A male toad is a platform artist (the female does not sing); he likes to hop on some object above the water line when he wishes to sing his *chanson d'amour*. It is during this time that toads select their mates and egg laying takes place.

After their spawning period is over, toads soon leave the water and spread out over the land, where they feed mostly on insects and earthworms. They rest in the shade in daytime and come out in the evening to find food. A toad's normal span of life is many years, perhaps twenty or more—long enough to do away with a fantastically large number of insects.

The American toad comes out in the evening to feed on insects and earthworms.

The male toad blows up his throat to immense proportions as he sings his mating song.

The female, while under the grasp of the male, extrudes into the water her long strings of eggs. The male immediately covers the eggs with sperm to fertilize them.

In a few days, tiny black tadpoles begin to hatch from the eggs. At first they have a heavy body and a long, thin tail.

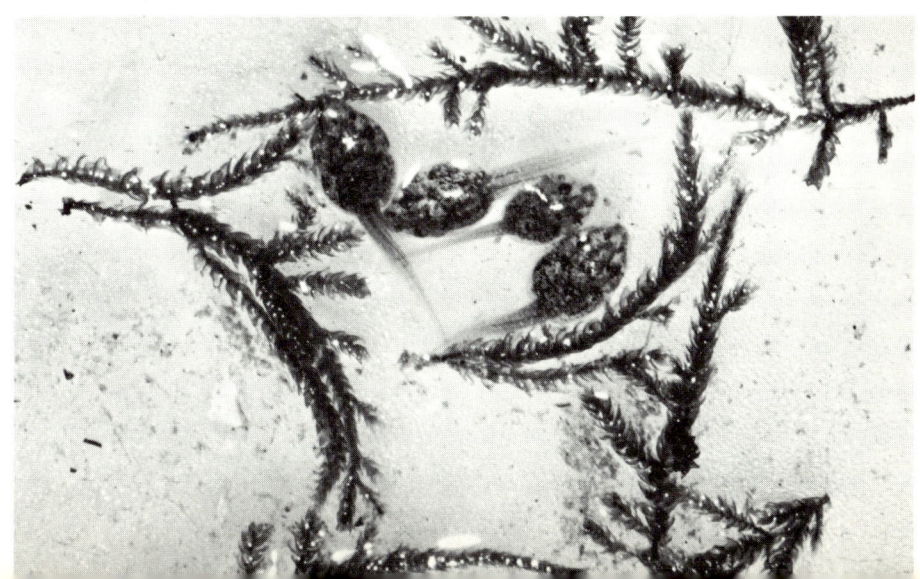

A tadpole lives in water and breathes with gills. Gradually it changes into a toad, with lungs for breathing and legs for hopping.

A toad leaves the water as an immature adult, measuring only about an inch in length. It is full-grown in two years.

Leopard Frog
Rana pipiens

The cello artist among pond musicians is the leopard frog, recognized by the dark spots over the upper part of his body. The female has the same color but is the silent one. The call of the male is a group of deep cellolike notes sounding something like *au-au-au-auk*, produced under water as well as above.

To inflate his throat, the frog closes his mouth and nostrils, and forces air into the sacs by pulling in his stomach. Then suddenly he opens his nostrils, and as the voice sacs are deflated, he produces his familiar croak. The process is repeated for each call.

After the spawning season, which lasts only a few weeks, leopard frogs live in and out of the water. In the evening these frogs may be seen along banks of ponds and streams, where they feed on insects. They never venture very far away from water. In winter they hibernate in mud under water.

Leopard frog

Tree Frog
Hyla versicolor

The tree frog, commonly called a tree toad, leads a varied life through the four seasons of the year. During the cold winter months it hibernates in the ground, generally in the mud at the bottom of a pond. In the spring it lives for a few weeks in a shallow woodland pond during the mating season. It is at this time that the male inflates his throat to sing his trilling love song, while the female deposits her jellylike masses of eggs. After the eggs have been spawned, tree frogs go up into bushes and trees, where they feed on small insects until cool weather again sends them into hibernation.

A tree frog is difficult to locate in a tree. It sleeps during the brightest hours of the day with its body held closely against the tree bark. It holds itself in place with its toes, which are equipped with adhesive pads. Moreover, it can change its color to look like that of the bark on which it rests. Occasionally, before a rain, a tree frog will sing his familiar tree frog song from his arboreal perch.

Tree frog

Bullfrog
Rana catesbeiana

Tread lightly along the edge of a tree-rimmed pond in summer to see a big bullfrog. This corpulent and contented fellow is usually seen resting on his elbows with little more than his bulging eyes and big mouth showing above the water line.

The bullfrog is by far the largest and loudest member of any frog-pond chorus. As soon as he comes out of hibernation in the month of May, he announces his presence by his pond-splitting call of *chug-a-rum-m-m, more rum-m-m*. On a quiet night, his call can be heard a distance of a mile or more.

Approach a bullfrog too closely and it uses its powerful hind legs to send it headlong into the water. Scrambling downward and riling the water as it goes, a bullfrog is soon out of reach and out of sight under a blanket of mud.

Bullfrog

Salamanders

Salamanders, near relatives of toads and frogs, have tails throughout their lives. These amphibians, with few exceptions, have smooth, moist skins. Salamanders are often mistaken for lizards, but lizards have scales and claws on their toes. In contrast, salamanders do not have a scaly skin and they do not have clawed toes.

Young salamanders hatch from eggs laid in water or on land under rocks or in rotten wood. Eggs are laid singly, in strings, or in masses, depending on the species. Larval salamanders with gills hatch from the eggs and in due time change into adults. In some species the larval stage is completed inside the egg and then the salamander emerges as an adult. Some adult salamanders have gills and continue to live in water; others live on land and breathe with lungs; and still others breathe through their skin—they have neither gills nor lungs.

Salamanders are more plentiful than supposed, but because they are nocturnal, they are not readily seen in daytime. Look for salamanders in damp woodlands and along the edges of shallow streams from early spring until late fall. They come out at night to feed on insects and other small forms of life.

Red-backed Salamander
Plethodon cinereus

The red-backed salamander is a common species found in woodlands throughout the northeastern section of the United States. It hides in daytime in moist leaf mold, and under stumps and logs. At nighttime it comes out to find its food, consisting mainly of small insects.

This salamander, reaching four and a half inches in length, has two color phases. It has either a red or a gray band down its back. In the red phase, its sides are brown, gray, or black, while its under side is finely mottled with gray and white. In the gray phase, its body is mottled more or less throughout with gray and white.

The female clings upside down in her nesting cavity while depositing her eggs, which hang down like a little bunch of grapes. The larval stage is passed in the egg and the adults emerge already transformed into adults.

The woodland salamanders of the genus *Plethodon*, to which the red-backed species belongs, have neither gills nor lungs; they breathe through their moist skin.

Red-backed salamander

Long-tailed Salamander
Eurycea longicauda

This is one of our most beautiful salamanders. It averages five inches in length and has a long tail, as its name indicates.

Look for this salamander in cool rock-sheltered springs and along the edges of woodland brooks. Sometimes an old-fashioned springhouse meets its fancy. Its color above is bright orange-yellow, varied with small blue spots; its slender keeled tail is barred transversely with black.

The long-tailed salamander, like most salamanders, is nocturnal in its habits. It comes out at night to feed on mites, spiders, and small insects. It catches its prey with its long moist tongue that it flips out with remarkable speed.

The clusters of eggs laid in water in early spring hatch in a few days into tiny tadpolelike larvae that go through a period of living entirely in water before becoming adults.

Long-tailed salamander

Part 4

Woodland Birds (Aves)

Among the many creatures found in woodlands, the most colorful and accomplished are the birds. These feathered animals with beautiful colors and graceful actions include groups with such highly specialized abilities as flying, soaring, gliding, swimming, floating, diving, hopping, and perching.

Birds are superb songsters, singing their best songs in springtime, while mates are being selected, nests built, and fledglings reared. In building their nests, birds use instinctive skills that would challenge the best trained artisans. A few birds continue to sing throughout the year, apparently for the sheer enjoyment of singing.

In addition to their aesthetic value as songsters and actors, birds have long provided man with game, food, and feathers. Their most important economic role of all is surely that of destroying insects and rodents.

North American birds are generally divided into twenty orders, as follows: the large group of perching birds, the woodpeckers, the kingfishers, the trogons, the hummingbirds and swifts, the goatsuckers, the owls, the parrots, the cuckoos, the doves and pigeons, the gulls and shorebirds, the rails and cranes, the chickenlike birds (grouse, quails, and turkeys), the daytime hunters (falcons, hawks, and vultures), the ducks and geese, the long-legged waders (herons, bitterns, ibises, etc.), the pelicans and gannets, the petrels and albatrosses, the grebes, and the loons.

Song Sparrow
Melospiza melodia

The little song sparrow is found in all seasons of the year along the edges of woodland streams and in clearings where it can find grass seeds, its principal food.

In wintertime, as it creeps along on the ground, the song sparrow talks to itself in muffled tones. Then suddenly, as spring approaches, it flies to the topmost branch of a shrub, throws back its head and sings its sweetest song, described by Thoreau as *"Maids! maids! maids! hang up your teakettle-ettle-ettle."* You will know this little sparrow by its brown-streaked breast with a black brooch pinned at the center.

The nest of the song sparrow, a dainty cuplike structure, is usually hidden in a clump of grass or concealed in a weed stalk. The three to seven eggs it lays in the nest are greenish-white, with many red-brown spots.

The song sparrow is a friendly little songster, identified by its brown-streaked breast with a large brown irregular, spot. It sings in all kinds of weather.

The song sparrow's nest, built of dried grass, is hidden in clumps of vegetation, low bushes, and vines. The eggs are greenish-white, spotted with red-brown.

Indigo Bunting
Passerina cyanea

The male indigo bunting, a persistent summer songster with high-pitched whistled notes, is easily identified by his rich blue color from head to foot. You see him flying through open spaces from tree to tree along woodland edges. But what a surprise when you become acquainted with the other members of his family.

The female indigo bunting, a shy sparrowlike bird, has no prominent markings at all; the fledglings, both male and female, are even less colorful. The young males gradually acquire deep blue feathers with their adulthood.

Indigo buntings build their nests in low-growing bushes, away from direct observation. However, the general location of the nest is usually given away by the male, who keeps a watchful eye from a nearby perch. There he sings his best from a topmost branch of a tree with the clear blue sky overhead.

A favored location for a nest is in a blackberry bush bordering a woods. The nest, well constructed of grasses and animal hairs, contains from three to four bluish-white eggs, incubated by the female.

Three dull-colored baby indigo buntings.

A baby bunting out on a limb waiting for something to eat.

Junior opens wide as mother bunting begins to feed him a buzzing bug.

Mother bunting forces the big fat bug all the way down Junior's throat.

Ovenbird
Seiurus aurocapillus

Go into the woods about the time the mountain laurel is in bloom to hear the shrill, emphatic song of the ovenbird. *Tea-cher, tea-cher, tea-cher* the bird calls as it picks its way through the underbrush. Sit down quietly for awhile to see the ovenbird calmly walking over the forest floor or stepping daintily along the top of a fallen log, bobbing its head and tail as it moves along. When disturbed it quickly flies into a bush or a low-growing tree some distance away.

The ovenbird, about the size of a song sparrow, is olive-brown above with a black-bordered golden crown and a white eyeline. Its breast is heavily streaked with black and white, and its legs and feet are pink. The ovenbird is found in woodlands extending from the Atlantic coast westward through Nebraska.

The ovenbird builds its nest by slipping twigs and grass under a mound of leaves. Arched on top with a side entrance, it resembles an old-fashioned oven, from which comes this wood warbler's odd name of ovenbird. About the only time an ovenbird's nest is found is when its location is revealed by the brooding bird. When disturbed she flutters away, wings and tail dragging as if she were injured—a pathetic pose intended only as a ruse to lure you away.

The photographer caught this ovenbird standing in front of her Dutch-oven nest.

Wood Thrush
Hylocichla mustelina

One of the sweetest songsters in all America is the wood thrush. Look for this distinguished songbird along woodland trails where crowns of tall trees merge and lacy ferns line your pathway.

Come upon a wood thrush suddenly and it will announce its alarm with an emphatic *pit, pit, pit.* It usually eyes you long enough for you to see its cinnamon-brown coat dappled with brown on breast and sides. Then off it flies into deeper woods. There, in the hush of evening, it sings its sweetest song—flutelike opening notes of *ee-o-lee* that gradually increase in quality until the refrain reaches its sweetest *nolee-aeolee-lee.*

The wood thrush builds its nest ten feet above the ground in the forks of heavy bushes or sturdy saplings. Building material consists of twigs, leaves, bark fiber, and a small amount of damp leaf mold. After the nest is dry and firm, it is carefully lined with fine rootlets and grasses. The female incubates the eggs, but both parents share in feeding the young. Frequently two broods are reared in a season.

Wood thrush

Brown Thrasher
Toxostoma rufum

The brown thrasher, larger than a robin, is identified by its cinnamon-brown color above, lighter color below, and dark brown streaks on its breast. The thrasher part of the bird's name comes from its habit of thrashing its long tail as it shyly moves about in shrubbery.

The song of the brown thrasher is a series of melodious phrases that it sings from the upper branches of a tall tree. The song is somewhat like that of its cousin, the mockingbird, except that each phrase is repeated only twice, and fewer imitations of other songsters are included. The alarm note is a loud kissing sound, unlike that of any other bird.

The brown thrasher spends much of its time on the ground searching in thickets for such food as beetles, caterpillars, and grasshoppers. It also feeds on many kinds of fruits and berries.

A favorite nesting place for a brown thrasher is in the low dense foliage of a hawthorn bush. The nest is roughly built from twigs, rootlets, and leaves. Three to six light-colored eggs, thickly dotted with red-brown, are laid in the nest. The parent birds are extremely devoted to their young and will defend them furiously in the face of imminent danger.

The mother brown thrasher sticks to her nest when her young appear to be threatened.

A young brown thrasher about to try its wings for the first time.

The handsome father bird keeps a watchful eye on his family.

Tufted Titmouse
Parus bicolor

In energy and inquisitiveness, few birds can equal the little tufted titmouse measuring barely six inches in length. You hear its happy-go-lucky whistled tune, *pe-to, pe-to, pe-to,* from the treetops, which cannot be mistaken for any other bird.

As the little songster moves closer, you see its mousy-gray color, its crested head with sides washed with orange, and its black feet and bill. This active little busybody is usually seen swinging on a tree limb, peering with beady eyes for a morsel of food.

During the winter when its daily fare of seeds and insects is scarce, the tufted titmouse is readily attracted to a feeding tray outside a window. The little bird wings in frequently, eyes you momentarily, and then grabs a seed and flies away with it to a nearby tree branch. There the titmouse holds the seed under its toes against the branch while it pounds away with its short, sharp beak until it can reach the tasty kernel.

Tufted titmouse

American Crow
Corvus brachyrhynchos

The American crow is a common year-round resident of field and forest throughout most of the United States. Frequently a flock of these big, black, bold birds are seen in a cornfield, where they post guards to be on the lookout for an irate farmer with a shotgun. At the first hint of danger, the sentinels croak out an alarm and quickly a black cloud of crows rises from the ground, sweeps across the open field, and disappears in the nearest woods.

Crows do eat some corn, but on the other hand, they gobble up huge quantities of destructive bugs and worms. They also are useful scavengers; they'll eat practically anything—either plant or animal—that is edible.

A crow's nest, a bulky structure, is built of sticks and twigs high up in a tree—usually too high for a boy to easily climb up and pick out a young crow for a pet.

Adult American crow

Yellow-shafted Flicker
Colaptes auratus

A woods in spring is filled with the mate-calling and home-drilling of the friendly, flirting flicker. The song includes a number of joyous variations of this woodpecker's loud, clear, many-times-repeated *wick, wick, wick*. This flicker has a slaty-gray head marked on the back with a bright red spot. It wears a golden-brown coat shading to gray and barred with black. Its stylish brownish-white vest is trimmed at the top with a velvety black crescent. The male always sports a black mustache. Even the babies, both male and female, grow mustaches. Fortunately the females lose theirs as they grow up. The golden lining of the flicker's tail and wings flashes in the sunlight as it bounces away in undulating flight.

Young flickers are hatched on a mattress of chips in a tree cavity drilled out by woodpecker technique. The fledglings are fed "ant soup," partly digested ants, which the parents transfer from their crops to those of their young. Flickers feed almost exclusively on ants picked up on their long sticky tongues.

Yellow-shafted flicker

Ruby-throated Hummingbird
Archilochus colubris

A buzzing blur of wings and a flash of iridescent green tells you that a rubythroat is nearby probing into bell-shaped flowers for nectar and tiny insects. This feathered midget, weighing only about a tenth of an ounce, approaches a flower on fast-beating wings, hovers in mid-air a few seconds, then extends its long tongue deep into the flower for refreshment. When ready to leave, it first goes into reverse to remove its long beak from the blossom. In the next action, it swings into high and hurries on to the next inviting flower. The male has a ruby patch on his throat, which is missing on the female.

A rubythroat's nest, saddled on a tree limb, is built of such fairy things as spider webs and plant down, and stuccoed on the outside with green moss and gray lichens. From the two tiny white eggs laid in the nest, two ill-shaped fledglings are hatched, which the mother feeds by pumping predigested food into their crops.

By late fall, the young are full-grown and strong enough to migrate, as all rubythroats do, all the way to Central America, including a 500-mile nonstop flight across the Gulf of Mexico. In the following spring, the rubythroats will return to their native homeland extending as far north as Canada.

A ruby-throated hummingbird hovering in mid-air.

The hummingbird nest, built on a tree limb, contains two white eggs. Young hummingbirds are full-grown in about three weeks—and constantly hungry!

Screech Owl
Otus asio

The little screech owl, not much larger than a robin, likes to live in open woods where mice and insects are readily found for food during its nighttime flying excursions. Among the dozen species of owls found in the United States, the screech owl is the one most frequently seen. Sometimes you will find it in broad daylight sitting half asleep on a tree limb. When disturbed, it opens its big round, yellow eyes and stares directly at you.

The screech owl is unusual in that it is found, for no particular reason known, in two color phases. Its feathers, either gray or reddish brown, are marked with black and delicately flecked with yellowish white. Prominent ear tufts and big staring eyes give the owl a ghoulish look.

An owl has eyes that are fixed in their sockets. It must, therefore, stare when it looks at you, and turn its head as it looks from one place to another. This accounts for the absurd belief that you can make an owl twist its head off by walking around it. What the owl actually does in such a case is to snap its head quickly around and pick up the view from the opposite side of its body. The screech owl does not screech, as its name implies, but when night approaches, you may hear its mournful call.

Screech owl

Barn Owl
Tyto alba

Sometimes in a woods at dusk, you will see a big shadowy creature flying swiftly on muffled wings. This is the elusive barn owl, found on every continent of the world. No other bird, so widely distributed, is so seldom seen at close range. When located and cornered, occasionally in an old building, the barn owl has the habit of leaning forward on its long legs and swinging its weird monkeylike face from side to side. Its call, usually uttered in flight, is a hissing scream, uncanny and ghostly.

With a wing spread of over three feet and feathers edged with down for silent flying, the barn owl finds its food while flying in early morning and in the evening. In catching prey, it uses its powerful needle-sharp claws, hooked and pointed.

Barn owls nest in hollow trees. Occasionally a nest is found in an old barn where mice and rats are plentiful. The female, nesting as early as March, lays her white eggs at two- to eight-day intervals and starts incubating as soon as the first egg is laid. As a result, the young are graded in age, as well as in size—a comic lot.

Young owls are covered with snow-white down until they grow their adulthood feathers. They have enormous appetites and will eat their own weight in food each night if they can get it. Small rodents are bolted whole, while larger ones are torn apart by the parents before being fed to the young. Bones and fur are formed into large pellets and then regurgitated by owls.

This barn owl placed her nest in an old chimney.

A nest of young barn owls.

Sparrow Hawk
Falco sparverius

  The sparrow hawk is a handsome little hawk, not much larger than a robin, frequently seen perched in a tall tree where a lookout is provided. It has a narrow, reddish tail tipped with a band of black and white, and a blue-gray head marked with black. Its long, pointed wings classify this little hawk with the falcons.

  Searching for mice and grasshoppers, the sparrow hawk maneuvers over open fields, sometimes hovering on slow-beating wings, while peering down with its marvelously developed telescopic eyes. When prey is sighted, perhaps a mouse, the hawk dives to the ground and makes the catch with its sharp talons. The prey is carried away to a favorite perch where it is torn apart and eaten in pieces. In winter when food is scarce, hunger may force this hawk to prey on small birds.

  Sparrow hawks nest in tree cavities, usually discarded woodpecker holes found in shade, orchard, and woodland trees. The four to five eggs in a nest are white, tinted with red and splotched with brown.

A sparrow hawk in juvenile feathers.

A young sparrow hawk just learning to fly.

The author and his pet sparrow hawk talk things over.

Mallard Duck
Anas platyrhynchos

The mallard, a common duck throughout most of North America, has for centuries furnished eggs, meat, and feathers for man. It readily adjusts itself to almost any environment and is the ancestor of most domesticated ducks.

The nest, usually located on the ground, is built from grasses, leaves, and rootlets. It is lined with downy feathers the mother duck plucks from her own breast. In this warm bed, the female lays ten to twelve pale olive-colored eggs.

Nature provides that all the eggs hatch within an hour or so of one another so that all of the brood may head for the water at the same time under the mother's guidance. When danger threatens, the mother quickly lowers her head and "freezes" on the spot. Her fledglings also know how to keep still when signaled to do so, to escape the sharp eyes of predators. Young ducks swim with ease as soon as they reach water.

In autumn great flocks of mallards begin to fly south from the northern breeding grounds. Eager hunters are waiting for these "green heads," as they are called from the bright green head of the drake. At first sight of a hunter, the ducks spring from the water at a bound and go whistling through the air at fifty or more miles per hour.

When cornered, this mother mallard duck did not fly away. Instead, she lowered her head and "froze" as if attempting to hide herself. Even the ducklings seemed to know to keep still when signaled by the mother duck to do so.

Adult mallards—two females and a drake.

Mallards "tipping up" to feed in shallow water.

Canada Goose
Branta canadensis

A beautiful sight in spring and again in autumn is a flock of Canada geese flying high overhead in V-formation. The flock always announces its appearance by the loud and discordant honking of the members. In flight, these geese are directed by a trusted leader that guides the group, not with compass, but with that mysterious power known as migratory impulse.

In spring when the geese reach their nesting grounds, from the northern part of the United States and into Canada, they settle down in grassy areas along streams and lakes. The nest is nothing more than a down-lined pile of sticks placed on dry land, usually near the water on a grassy elevation. The gander, a very faithful mate, usually for many years, stands at the nest while his mate broods the eggs. The five to nine buff-white eggs hatch in about a month. As soon as the yellow goslings step out of their shells and their birthday suits are dry, they are ready to swim like old timers. The whole family takes to the water at the same time, under the leadership of the gander. When danger threatens the youngsters dive under water. Parents and young feed on a variety of aquatic plants. On land they pick up tender shoots of grasses and an occasional grasshopper. The parents never put food in the mouths of the goslings. Food is pointed out to them but they pick it up on their own. While the young are growing up, the old birds molt, then by fall all have strong wing feathers—strong enough to carry them to their winter feeding areas southward throughout the United States.

The Canada goose, reaching a length of forty inches, has a brownish gray body, with a black head and neck. A prominent identifying mark is the white chin strap on its long, black neck.

So instinctive is the urge to fly in V-formation, that a flock will sometimes go into formation before leaving the water.

Fortunately, a friendly boy found this stranded goose that had fallen out of formation from sheer exhaustion. After food and water and a day's rest, it was ready to continue on its migratory journey.

Green Heron
Butorides virescens

Of the many common names given the green heron, the one that fits it best is "little-fly-up-the-creek." At the first hint of danger, this clever little fisherman, often with a fish in its beak, gives out a noisy squawk as it flaps its way around the willow bend and into the distance.

In fishing along the edge of a stream, the green heron hardly causes a ripple as it wades slowly through the water. When a fish or some other choice morsel is sighted, this droll-looking bird uses its sharp beak with accurate aim. If the catch is a fish, it is deftly flipped around so that it can be swallowed head first without danger of sharp fins cutting its tender throat.

The nest of a green heron is little more than a platform of sticks placed in a bush or a tree near the water. From four to six greenish-blue eggs are hatched into fuzzy, ugly fledglings. At first young herons are feeble and inactive, but on a diet of fish, frogs, and insects, they grow rapidly. Soon they are strong enough to scramble out of their jerry-built nest and perch securely on their big yellow feet. Like this one, young herons when disturbed will stretch their long necks upward and stand for a few minutes as still as a statue.

Green heron

Great blue heron

Great Blue Heron
Ardea herodias

The great blue heron, distinguished for its sharp pointed bill, its long slender neck, and its storklike legs, stands motionless in shallow water until a fish or frog comes within striking distance. Then with lightning speed, it thrusts its head into the water and comes up with the catch. If a fish is speared that is too big and lively to be immediately swallowed, it is taken to land, flailed into helplessness and then swallowed headfirst. Approach too closely and suddenly this graceful heron takes to the air on splendid, slow-beating wings.

Great blue herons nest in colonies year after year in groves of tall swampland trees. The birds, arriving in early spring, build their nests, and rear their young. The nests are large, unsightly bowl-shaped structures built high up in trees from small branches, twigs, and dry grass. Often an old nest is repaired. Two to six white eggs are hatched into ill-shaped and helpless youngsters. In feeding the young, a parent bird stands at the edge of the nest and pumps semi-digested food into each gaping mouth. In the fall, after the family is reared, great blue herons leave their treetop homes to resume their solitary wanderings.

Index

Asterisk (*) indicates photograph

Albatross, 87
Amphibian, 70, 71, 83
Anas platyrhynchos, 118
Archilochus colubris, 107
Ardea herodias, 125
Artiodactyl, 11
Aves, 87

Bat, 11
  big brown, 43, *44, *45
Birds, chickenlike, 87
  classification of, 87
  perching, 87
Bobcat, 11, 32, *33
Branta canadensis, 121
Bufo terrestris, 72
Bullfrog, 81, *82
Bunting, indigo, 90, *91–93
Butorides virescens, 123

Canis lupus, 36
Carapace, 63
Carnivora, 11
Chelydra serpentina, 68
Chickaree, 23
Chipmunk, eastern, 27, *28
Chiroptera, 11
Clemmys muhlenbergi, 66
Colaptes auratus, 105
Condylura cristata, 46
Constrictor, 52
Copperhead, 51, 56
Coral snake, 51
Corvus brachyrhynchos, 103
Cottonmouth, 51
Crane, 87
Crocodile, 50
Crow, American, 103, *104
Cuckoo, 87

Deer, 11
  white-tailed, 12, *13

Diadophis punctatus, 54
Didelphis marsupialis, 48
Dove, 87
Duck, 87
  mallard, 118, *119–120, *122

Elaphe obsoleta, 52
Eptesicus fuscus, 43
Eumeces fasciatus, 61
Eurycea longicauda, 86

Falco sparverius, 114
Flicker, yellow-shafted, 105, *106
Fox, 11
  gray, 34, *35
  red, 34
Frog, 71
  leopard, 77, *78
  tree, 77, *80

Gannet, 87
Geese, 87
Glaucomys volans, 21
Goat, 11
Goatsucker, 87
Goose, Canada, 121, *122
Grebe, 87
Groundhog, 29
Groundhog Day, 29
Gull, 87

Hare, 14
Hawk, sparrow, 114, *115–117
Hedgehog, 29
Heron, blue, *125
  green, 123, *124
Heterodon platyrhinos, 56
Hibernation, 29, 43, 50, 56, 62, 64, 71, 77, 79, 81
Hudson seal, 18
Hummingbird, 87
  ruby-throated, 107, *108–9
Hunters, daytime, 87

Hyla versicolor, 79
Hylocichla mustelina, 96

Iguana, 61
Insectivora, 11

Kangaroo, Australian, 48
Kingfisher, 87
Kit, 32

Lagomorpha, 11
Leveret, 14
Lizard, 50, 61, 83
    fence, 61, *62
Loon, 87
Lynx, bay, 32
    Canadian, 32
Lynx canadensis, 32
Lynx rufus, 32

Mammals, 11
Marmota monax, 29
Marsupial, 48
Marsupialia, 11
Melospiza melodia, 88
Mephitis mephitis, 38
Mice, 11
Microtus pennsylvanicus, 16
Mole, common, 11, 46
    star-nosed, 46, *47
Mouse, field, 16
    house, 20
    meadow, 16
        white-footed, *19, 20
Muhlenberg, Dr. H. E., 66
Mus musculus, 20
Muskrat, 11, 18, *19

Odocoileus virginianus, 12
Ondatra zibethicus, 18
Opossum, 11, 48, *49
Otus asio, 110
Ovenbird, 94, *95
Owl, 11
    barn, 112, *113–114
    screech, 110, *111

Parrot, 87
Parus bicolor, 101
Passerina cyanea, 90
Pelican, 87
Peromyscus leocopus, 20
Petrel, 87
Pigeon, 87
Plastron, 63
Plethodon cinereus, 84
Procyon lotor, 41

Rabbit, 11
    cottontail, eastern, 14, *15
    jack, 14
Raccoon, 11, *40, 41, *42
Rail, 87
Rana catesbeiana, 81
Rana pipiens, 77
Rattlesnake, 51
Reptile, 50, 51
Reptilia, 50
Rodentia, 11

Salamander, 83
    long-tailed, *86
    red-backed, 84, *85
Scalopus aquaticus, 46
Sceloporus undulatus, 61, 62
Sciurus carolinensis, 25
Seiurus aurocapillus, 94
Sheep, 11
Shorebirds, 87
Shrew, 11
Skink, five-lined, 61
Skunk, 11, 64
    striped, 38, *39
Snake, black rat, 52, *53, *54
    hognose, 56, *57–60
    ringneck, 54, *55
Snakes, 50, 51
    poisonous, 51

Index

Sparrow, song, 88, *89
Squirrel, 11
 flying, *21, *22
 gray, *25, *26
 red, 23, *24
Swift, 87
Sylvilagus floridanus, 14

Tamiasciurus hudsonicus, 23
Tamias striatus, 27
Terrapene carolina, 64
Terrapin, 63
Thoreau, 88
Thrasher, brown, 98, *99–100
Thrush, wood, 96, *97
Titmouse, tufted, 101, *102
Toad, 71
 American, 72, *73–76
Tortoise, 63
Toxostoma rufum, 98

Trogon, 87
Turtle, 50, 63
 bog, 66, *67
 box, 63, 64, *65
 Muhlenberg, 66
 snapping, 68, *69
Tyto alba, 112

Urocyon cinereoargenteus, 34

Vole, 11
 meadow, 16, *17
Vulpus fulva, 34

Waders, long-legged, 87
Woodchuck, 11, 29, *30, *31
Woodpecker, 87
Wolf, gray, 36, *37
 timber, 36